Icarus

Israel Colón

TOHO
PUBLISHING

To Linda Golden-Rigby:

*You saw something in me that I could not,
so my way of saying thank you
is by doing everything
you said I could.*

*These words are for the time you told me,
"You got a book in you."*

*Well, much like everything else you said I could,
I did.*

*Love,
Izzy*

CONTENTS

6	Icarus
8	Fate
9	Involuntary Wings
11	The Moon and Me
13	December 26, 2005
16	Nameless
17	Revolver
18	6 lbs., 9 oz.
20	I Didn't Say "No"
22	As Fate Would Have It
23	A Shot in the Dark
24	Tickling Tide
26	The Moon Has Died
28	Luna's Rose
30	Leaving September
31	Dirty Knees
33	A Hero's Pain
34	Voyager I

ICARUS

Occasionally,
the mind hosts
a dream

between sequences
of
screaming nights.

Sweat fuels
restless sleep
as

grinding teeth
engine feet,
teasing flight.

Corneas scrape lids
while I cautiously
scan the sky.

(Hoping I'm in bed)
I raise my chin
and fly.

Landing enters thought,
after opening
sunburnt eyes.

Shaken by the inevitable,
unsure
if I took a risk and tried.

Now, I'll count
possibilities
I do deny.

A feel it is to be free,
but am I
even alive?

FATE

It seems sister caught a scratch
(the only rationale we had left)
causing uncle to seek justice
as we chose to pray for the best.

Fate, surely at fault,
but too loved to take blame,
so the lives she sprung (oh so young)
were all that remained to be slain.

A poker swung and boot crushed lungs
lead to dirt displaced in the yard.
Faint meows echoed the house
with snaps of bones left shard.

The infection would pass (prompting a gasp)
as there were fewer left to pet.
The kittens weren't gone, but in the lawn,
of the house their mother kept.

INVOLUNTARY WINGS

It was many a year ago,
       outside the city where she used to breathe.
Her age unchanged though moons have passed.
       That night the moon brought her killer to me.

Won't speak his name as it won't change . . .
       No, it won't change a thing.
My thoughts still wander as I stew and ponder
       why a demon brought Deanna her wings.

No one knew that Deanna flew
       until her messenger decided to speak.
To my uncle's surprise, he shared his secret,
       and my uncle shared this secret with me.

This is the reason her family knows
       she isn't missing, but ceases to be.
Through faithful eyes I look inside
       for the reason she had to leave.

The demon does his time, as I do mine,
       in the city where she used to breathe.
No more searching the town, Deanna's been found
       in the place God wants her to be.

God, would you please speak to the events
        that occurred December 4th, 2004?

Either he's not there or too busy to share
        what Deanna Wright McIntosh died for.

THE MOON AND ME

The sun gives chase.
I waste . . .
away counting sheep.

Creep out the door,
eyes to skies,
hoping something's watching me.

There's nothing new.
No secret shared.
Just the moon that I can see.

I say hello
and watch it go
to a place I'd rather be.

It's ruthless
being lucid,
rougher wrangling why.

The sun will rise,
I'll say goodbye
to a moon that leaves the sky.

My spirit burns.
I wait my turn,
until the time to leave is mine.

DECEMBER 26, 2005

He was a child,
and so was I.
Of him I think, still,

till this day.

With every December
I guiltily remember
the boy who gave his life for me.

Defenseless,

in that place he loved to be.
It was only a bridge ride away
(yet felt closer to home than what was).

Seven children,

but monsters saw a man in me.
An unlocked door invited them four,
and with force we welcomed their greed.

Tearlessly,
a child laid down his life
while listening to a tear-ridden soundtrack

of duct tape ripped and pulsating pain.

Fear caught my eye,

as the girls gave me theirs,
surrendering every bit of lost hope
to someone I knew was a stranger.

The boy prayed,

not of another day,
nor the chance of miracles,
but that the girls' innocence would stay.

Something persevered

within the boy whose self was lost.
So bound at ankle and wrist, I took a risk
and licked away the tape against my lips.

I bit that fucking tape.

As dry teeth scraped new skin
a body, foreign, was now freed;
but face down, head draped in an old towel, that
        boy remained.

What a loss was had

as only six children walked away,
greeting grieving parents across a caution line.
No one noticed the boy who gave his life.

It isn't right

that no funeral was had,
none sobbing by candlelight.
That beautiful boy was buried nameless.

It hurts to remember him

knowing that I was he who put him away.
Humanity was lost in the place I left him,
and I'm the only one who knows

the boy who died was me.

NAMELESS

No life to etch my tomb,
but still and soon so be my will.
None left to kill so left in time,
too tired, for I, this hole to fill.

Questions mark the grave on through,
for simply 'tis a nameless stone.
Hammer laid, chisel, too;
none came to make this dirt my home.

Alas, this rest of mine came true.
If thought had I and strength to name,
this rock for all the passers through,
but sleep swept fast and no one came.

If time had I to think this out,
or will to sprout and mark my grave
with all the frills and flowers, too,
by myself it'd be, thus it's all the same.

Half-closed lies the casket.
A weak hand bears the blame.
Marked simply by unfinished stone.
Still unfinished, because no one came.

REVOLVER

My hand is a gun.
It wants to keep the peace.
Never mind the posturing.

My hand is a gun.
My shoulder is weak,
but I won't put it down.

My hand is a gun
indexed at me.
Can't I let it go?

My gun is a hand;
soft and outreached,
forged in shade of blue.

6 LBS., 9 OZ.

I want out.
Can't begin to count
the numerous times
I've put steel
in my mouth.

Eyes won't sleep.
The rage pouring
causes drought.
I drink it down with the thought
that I want out.

So tonight, the bottle
races the trigger.
I figure either way
I won't stay to see the sun
as the morning sprouts.

Somehow tomorrow won,
and I'm glad it did.
because I have news,
and reason to live.
The boy who died is having a kid.

I'm having a kid,
and she'll never know
the places that I've been.
I doubt that I want out,
but don't know my way in.

I DIDN'T SAY "NO"

"How are you, really?"

> "You see, I don't know."

"But, really, how are you?"

> "Without the time for feeling to show."

"How are you doing?"

> (A loving hand caresses me slow.)
> "I'm doing the best that I can."

"Tell me what it is that hurts you so."

> "I can't explain the numbing pain."

"But can you let it go?"

> "It's all I know, my only home . . . "

"And now it's time to grow."

> "If it leaves it'll leave me . . .
> Well, I'll be left alone."

"Alone with pain leaves you the same.
You've made friend of former foe.
I'll guide you if you're ready—"

(a familiar voice interrupts)
"No!"

AS FATE WOULD HAVE IT

More time has passed; dirt grew to grass.
The summer had just begun,
but uncle wasn't there to spare the guilty,
so, by default, I was the one.

Like frightened fur I made him shed,
without a pick nor boots, just I.
Lured him with pain, and so he came,
to the yard with kittens to die.

Consciousness crept so I rained,
personal storm of fist and knee.
Again he slept, my mother wept,
before his breath, what left was me.

The urge was great but sealed was fate.
Broken was the curse from a tug.
Not force nor fright, but 'twas the night
that this became the house of love.

A SHOT IN THE DARK

For if you find me with a gun,
do not be scared, do not run.

There only lies a single shot.
This has to work (it's all I got).

Let this shot be so precise
that it may take me

but not my life.

TICKLING TIDE

I can't help but to wonder
why the water is so dense between us
(thrashing against my will),

but still and always,
I kill myself as if it's for you,
but reality strikes.

If you were to leave,
somehow I'll never know.
I'm sure time will get the best of me

allowing to drift my memory,
Overflowing with remnants of you
beating against the coast.

Though scars aren't much to boast
it's all that's left and true.
Shrines scattered across the burning sands

a flame that's yet undo.
Oceans tattered,
rippling waves

barely sustaining the pain on through;
mirroring me (tense),
dense as the water is blue.

THE MOON HAS DIED

For once I will sleep a rest
so easy as if I didn't try.
My chest breathes lighter.
It seems the moon has died.

Lessons may have their hold
making way for clearer skies.
My eyes linger far closer now.
It seems the moon has died.

I know little of forever,
far more of you and I.
You've been floating in the way.
It seems the moon has died.

We've gone through this before,
and seen so many goodbyes.
I guess I'm too happy to dwell.
It seems the moon has died.

I've asked the stars to move,
so you could have a moment to shine.
The world will watch in awe because
it seems the moon has died.

"The moon has died! The moon has died."
My moon, it went and died.
Seems like you made the front page,
once we were out of time.

LUNA'S ROSE

Perhaps I knew it would be like this.
Maybe that's why I waited,
so that she could hold you first,
to no avail;
initial attempt to break the curse.

It felt like forever,
waiting to mix your smell with mine,
but there was nothing more I wanted to see
than my daughter and her mother,
with my own eyes.

This isn't the first time
I saw a silhouette fade.
But unlike before,
it wasn't mine
that was walking away.

You stole six weeks,
never missing a beat,
and with that you almost never were,
and your mommy almost died,
and she almost made it, too.

When your eyes meet mine,
with our hearts in hands,
you can have certainty,
you can have peace,
even though, often,
I know not what I do.

Yes, for you I will burn
a world through,
loving until you run away,
because I know that you will,
to someone like your dad.

LEAVING SEPTEMBER

If a time box surrounded our days,
I'm sure yours is as rough as mine.
Time is hard keeping on so, if you could,
just tell me everything will be fine.

Stains you made haven't dulled
from when you "spilled" unopened wine.
I found a shard of glass weeks ago,
where wet pills rolled when you tried leaving it
behind.

Before the police came you took photos of your
        neck,
so I assume that saving your life was a crime.
Without bruises you'd have no breath for excuses,
        nor warm lips
to kiss our daughter every time you say goodbye.

Maybe one day you won't resent me when you see
        her,
and perhaps even I can get better in time.
I know that everything works itself out in the end,
but won't someone just tell me everything will be fine?

DIRTY KNEES

Whether it be
from the storm
or me,
I'm simply
weathered.

If perhaps there's
a tether,
could we
start anew,
together?

Make these
roaring whispers
something
I can
see.

I'm scared
(up there)
I'll be unaware,
or left alone
with me.

Artificial control
takes a toll.
(I need something
to
believe).

Excuse my time away.
If you're here
I'll stay,
and honestly
I'm too tired to leave.

When I went, I spent
all that I had
so, I crawled
to where
I used to be.

I've changed my stance,
give me chance,
and judge me
for my
dirty knees.

A HERO'S PAIN

It was a good night, to see a good man.
Beers passed hands, as children played.
There was no need for a cape or theatrics.
Silent I stood as a hero danced away his pain.

Simple would it be to coin it a game.
With ease, he leaves all that left him tucked away.
In lieu of pleas for shadows to find form, his lips sing
a slurred rendition of song for us to stay.

Maybe God granted a heart that could endure,
a back to carry burdens like lint from morning
            through day,
but I dare not barter these moments with puzzled
            thoughts.
Silent I'll stand, as a hero sings away his pain.

It was a good night, for a good man.
I pray more find him on his way.
Some say to never meet your heroes,
but I'll stand, never looking away.

VOYAGER I

I love a pale-blue dot.
Remember this as I'm away.
I gave to you all that I had,
during the time that I could stay.

"I love you" created the blue.
"Adore" watered the green.
Everything I love is pale-blue,
floating on a golden beam.

If you could ask me why
all that I love is blue,
I'd reply, "A pale-blue dot is the world,
but, my love, my world is you."

ACKNOWLEDGEMENTS

To Andrés Cruciani, Josh Martin, Sean Hanrahan, Elijah Pringle, Ashley Rivera, Leena Taylor, Erica Abbott, Elisha Gibson, Eric "Neti Neti" Ammon, and Jonathan Koven—thank you for bringing the best out of me.

The members of the D.C. region of the Wounded Warrior Project—for giving me a sense of purpose.

My mother—for your love and support.

My father—for pushing me to shoot for the stars.

My daughters Elisa and Luna—for keeping me alive.

ABOUT THE POET

Israel Colón is a Philadelphia-based poet. Known for its inspired rhyme schemes and use of poetic form, Colón's work confronts his struggles with trauma, religion, and relationships. Through his mercilessly honest approach to writing, Colón shines a light on the experiences of a man barely keeping it together. His poetry most recently appeared in *Toho Journal: Duality (Vol. 2, No. 1)*.

Made in the USA
Middletown, DE
18 January 2021

31884167R00024